MACHINES RULE!

ON THE
RACE TRACK

Steve Parker

W
FRANKLIN WATTS
LONDON • SYDNEY

This edition 2012

First published in 2008
by Franklin Watts

Copyright © Franklin Watts 2008

Franklin Watts
338 Euston Road
London NW1 3BH

Franklin Watts Australia
Level 17/207 Kent Street
Sydney, NSW 2000

Editor: Jeremy Smith
Design: Billin Design Solutions
Art director: Jonathan Hair

Picture credits: Alamy: OFC main, 6, 8
all, 9tl, 13b, 13t, 26b, 27tr, 27b.
Corbis: 7t, 14 all, 15c, 16tr, 17tl, 17tr,
17b, 20, 21c, 24, 25b, 25tr, 27tl.
istockphoto: 7b, 10t, 21tl, 21tr, 25tl.
Shutterstock: OFC bl & br, 2, 3, 4, 7c,
9tr, 10b, 11 all, 12 all, 13tr, 15tr, 15b,
16b, 18, 19 all, 21b, 22, 23 all, 26t.

A CIP catalogue record for this book
is available from the British Library.

Dewey number: 629.47

ISBN: 978 1 4451 0930 5

Printed in China

Franklin Watts is a division of
Hachette Children's Books,
an Hachette UK company
www.hachette.co.uk

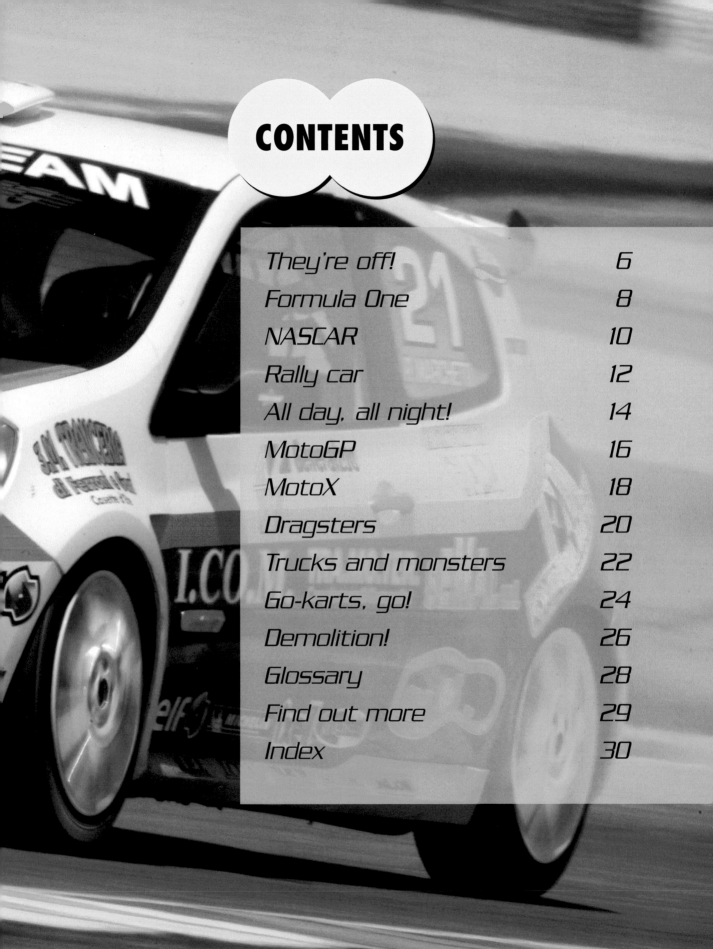

CONTENTS

They're off!

At the race track, the final is about to begin. The engines roar, the drivers are tense and ready, the flag waves as the lights change – and they're off! Lap after lap, the racers show their skills as they put their machines to the test. At the chequered flag, winner takes all!

F1 car
Nothing is faster around a twisty track than a Formula One (F1) car. As it brakes hard for the corner, then streaks away with a deafening whine, this vehicle is the ultimate racing machine. F1 is the richest, most famous, most glamorous racing in the world.

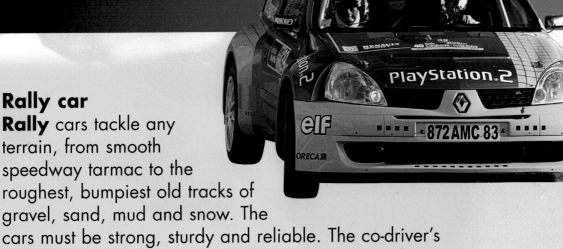

Rally car

Rally cars tackle any terrain, from smooth speedway tarmac to the roughest, bumpiest old tracks of gravel, sand, mud and snow. The cars must be strong, sturdy and reliable. The co-driver's map-reading skills are vital – no one wants to get lost!

Motorcycle

Swap four wheels for two, and you're riding a top Superbike or MotoGP motorcycle. Lean into the bend so your knees graze the track, then roar off down the straight, but keep the front wheel on the track – **wheelies** waste time!

Dragster

From a standing start, no racing machine picks up speed as fast as the dragster. Each race is ear-splitting and ground-shaking as two monster dragsters speed along the track. Both want to be first to flash past the finish line.

Formula One

Formula One, or F1, is the tops! No other car can beat an F1 machine for speed, handling, acceleration, braking and all-round racing action. And F1 has more spectators than any other motor sport.

Up to 20 F1 **Grand Prix** races are held each year around the world. The races are about 300 kilometres long and last up to two hours.

The driver's helmet has a radio in it which he uses to talk to his team at the trackside.

Typical F1 car

Length: 4.5 metres

Width: 1.8 metres

Height: 0.95 metre

Wheelbase: 3.1 metres

Weight: 600 kilograms on the start grid

Engine: 2.4 litres V8 (8 cylinder)

Power: 900-plus horsepower

Gears: 6 or 7, semi-automatic with paddle shift

Top speed: Over 320 km/h

During each race the cars go into the **pits** for new tyres, a refill of fuel and small repairs. It all takes less than 10 seconds.

THAT'S INCREDIBLE

During an F1 race, the driver loses more than 4 kilograms of body weight, mainly as sweat.

Dozens of electronic sensors in the F1 car gather information, from tyre pressure to how much fuel is left, and send it by radio to the team's many computers.

NASCAR

In North America, NASCAR races are the biggest. The National Association for Stock Car Auto Racing organises contests around giant arenas, watched by some of the world's biggest crowds.

Stock cars have a roll cage that protects the driver if there's a crash.

The cars are specially made versions of 'stock' cars, which are those sold for ordinary motoring.

The driver watches the dials on the dashboard to check for problems.

Typical NASCAR Sprint Cup stock car

Length: 4.8-5 metres

Width: About 1.9 metres

Height: 1.5 metres

Wheelbase: Around 2.8 metres

Weight: At least 1,545 kilograms with driver

Fuel tank: 67.2 litres

Engine: 5.8 litre V8 (8 cylinder)

Power: More than 750 horsepower

Gears: 4-speed manual

Top speed: 320 km/h

Track length: 850–4,280 metres

THAT'S INCREDIBLE

NASCAR draws crowds of up to 180,000 people. Tens of millions watch on TV, and there are 75 million regular fans.

Crashes happen all the time in NASCAR racing.

Rally car

Drivers roar up hills and often take off at the top. →

THAT'S INCREDIBLE
The longest, hardest motor race is the Dakar Rally. It is 10,000 kilometres long, and runs from European cities through to African deserts.

Like stock cars, rally cars are souped-up versions of ordinary cars. But rallying is the toughest motor sport. Drivers cope with lumps, bumps, mud, dirt, streams, snow, ice and much more, for three or four days!

Rally cars are 4WD (the engine turns all four wheels), giving great grip. ←

The driver sits in the left seat and the **navigator** in the right one. They are strapped in tight, and everything in the car is well padded.

Typical WRC car

Length: 4.3 metres

Width: 1.8 metres

Height: 1.5 metres

Wheelbase: 2.6 metres

Weight: At least 1,230 kilograms

Engine: 2 litres turbocharged

Power: Up to 350 horsepower

Gears: Usually 5

Top speed: 200 km/h

The World Rally Championship (WRC) puts on about 15 races in Europe, South America, Australia and New Zealand each year. Most are on tarmac roads but a couple are in snowy places such as Sweden and Norway.

all night!

To avoid getting tired, ordinary motorists should take a break every hour or two. Yet endurance car races run all day and all night – that's 24 hours at full speed!

The Le Mans 24-hour race has been taking place since 1923. →

THAT'S INCREDIBLE

The tradition of the winning driver spraying the crowd with fizzy champagne began at Le Mans with Dan Gurney in 1967!

Stats and Facts

Audi R8 (five-times Le Mans winner)

Length: 4.65 metres

Width: 2.0 metres

Height: 1.25 metres

Wheelbase: 2.73 metres

Weight: 911 kilograms basic

Engine: 3.6 litres V8, twin turbo

Power: About 600 horsepower

Gears: 6

Top speed: 340 km/h

Mechanics and engineers must be ready at any time for their car to come into the pits, even in the middle of the night.

Before the race, the car is taken apart, cleaned and every tiny part is checked to make sure it will last for 24 hours non-stop.

The Formula One of motorcycle racing is MotoGP, the Motorcycle Grand Prix series. These are bikes with amazing power and speed, breath-taking acceleration, heart-stopping brakes and the best all-round performance.

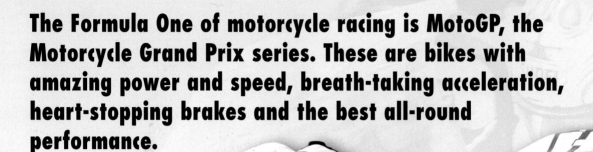

Racing motorcyclists lean into bends, their knees almost touching the ground, as they take the fastest route or 'racing line'.

Racing motorbikes have **disc brakes**.

Stats and Facts

Coloured flags are used in motor racing. A blue flag means a rider should let another racer overtake, for example, if the bike behind is more than a lap ahead of him.

Typical MotoGP bike such as Honda RC212V

Length: 2.05 metres

Width: 0.65 metres

Height: 1.13 metres

Wheelbase: 1.44 metres

Weight: 150 kilograms basic

Fuel: 21 litres

Engine: Up to 800 cc (0.8 litres)

Power: 200 horsepower

Front wheels: 406 mm diameter

Rear wheels: 419 mm diameter

Top speed: 347 km/h

THAT'S INCREDIBLE

For each race, including practice sessions, a MotoGP rider uses about 80 tyres. Each tyre costs hundreds of pounds!

Riders wear strong crash helmets and tough suits called 'leathers' for protection in crashes.

If you like dirt, mud, cold water, slips, slides, twists, bumps and shakes, all with the noisy whine of a motorbike engine – then MotoX is for you.

THAT'S INCREDIBLE
Some MotoX races are for riders as young as four years of age!

The front wheel is held in **forks** that can slide upwards as part of the **suspension**, to smooth out bumps and holes.

In MotoX (Motorcycle Cross Country or MX) the tracks have steep slopes where riders take off and 'fly' for many metres.

At the start, riders all roar off together.

FMX is Freestyle MotoX, where riders are judged on their jumps, stunts, tricks and skills.

Stats and Facts

Typical MotoX MX1 motorcycle

Length: 2.2 metres

Width: 0.8-0.9 metres

Height: 1.2-1.3 metres

Seat height: 0.8-1 metre

Wheelbase: 1.5 metres

Weight: 90-110 kilograms

Engine: 250 cc 2-stroke or 450 cc 4-stroke

Gears: 5

Fuel: 6-7 litres

Top speed: 152 km/h

Dragsters

No motor sport is as fast and loud as dragster racing. Yet there are only two cars each time, and they are in action for less than five seconds!

THAT'S INCREDIBLE
As the best dragsters blast past the finish line they are going more than 530 km/h!

A dragster race is on a straight track – 402.3 metres (a quarter of a mile) from the start to the finish line.

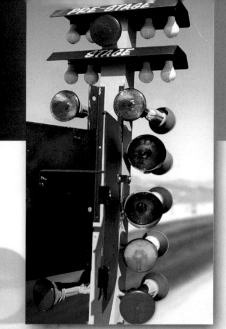

Stats and Facts

The countdown at the start line is shown by a series of coloured lights called a *Christmas Tree.*

Top Fuel Dragster

Category: Fastest type of dragster

Fuel: 9/10ths nitromethane, 1/10th methanol

Wheelbase: Between 4.57 and 7.62 metres

Height: Less than 2.3 metres to top of wing

Weight: At least 1,000 kilograms

Engine: Up to 8.2 litres

Power: More than 7,000 horsepower

Gears: 1

Top speed: Over 500 km/h at finish

There are several classes of dragster. Funny Cars look more like ordinary cars, but they still have massive rear tyres for super-**acceleration**.

Dragster engines have **supercharges** *on top.*

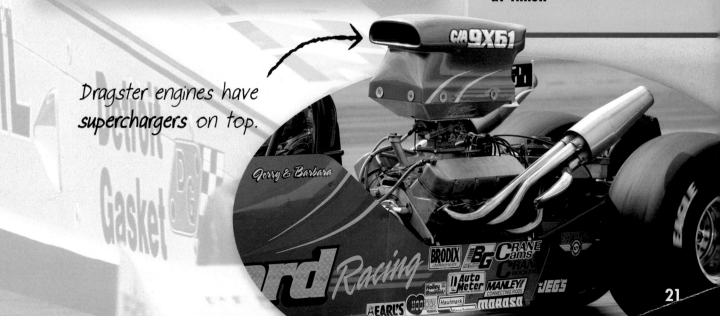

21

Trucks and monsters

For fun and thrills, as well as speed and power, why not visit the local speedway or racetrack when the Bigfoots and Monsters are in town?

THAT'S INCREDIBLE

Bigfoot number 14 did a long jump of almost 62 metres over a Boeing jet airliner!

Bigfoot trucks are specially built to look like normal pick-up trucks but with massive tyres. The first Bigfoot was built in 1975. Now there are more than 20 around the world, plus many similar-looking Monster trucks.

Stats and Facts

Big racing trucks have 12-litre turbocharged diesel engines.

Drivers gain points for their skills performing stunts like this wheelie, or for driving on the two wheels on the same side.

Pick-up trucks, specially modified for speed, can reach more than 200 km/h.

Bigfoot 17

Based on: Ford F150 Pick-Up Truck

Length: 5.5 metres

Width: 3.8 metres

Height: 3.1 metres

Weight: 4,200 kilograms

Engine: 11.4 litres Ford Racing V8

Power: 1,750 horsepower

Gears: 2

Tyre height: 1.67 metres

Top speed: 250 km/h

Go-karts, go!

Many world champion racers started on the kart track. Go-karts are small and simple, but they are also fast and nippy, and tricky to steer and brake. You need great skills to win a race.

Go-karts or karts are like mini racing cars, with an engine, gearbox and four tiny wheels. They are so low that even when driving slowly, it seems like you are zooming at high speed.

THAT'S INCREDIBLE

The fastest types of go-karts, Superkarts, can reach speeds of 250 km/h – more than twice the motorway speed limit!

Stats and Facts

The throttle (accelerator) pedal is on the right and the brake pedal on the left.

Drivers try to speed past on the straights and overtake on the inside at bends.

Typical KF1 (Formula A) kart

Length: Up to 1.82 metres

Width: Up to 1.4 metres

Height: Up to 0.65 metres (excluding seat)

Wheelbase: 1.01-1.07 metres

Weight: 75-80 kilograms basic, at least 156 kilograms with driver

Fuel tank: At least 8 litres

Engine: 125 cc

Gears: Continuous change (no separate gears)

Transmission: Chain and sprocket

Suspension: None

Top speed: 140 km/h

Demolition!

Old cars, or 'bangers', might rust away slowly in a garage or field. Or they might get crashed, smashed, crushed and destroyed in a Demolition Derby!

THAT'S INCREDIBLE

The Chrysler Imperial from the mid-1960s is so tough and strong that it's banned from many demolition and banger races because it would almost always win.

In the pits and paddock areas, the cars are unloaded from their trailers. Most have already been in bumps and scrapes.

Stats and Facts

On the track, survival is the key. Some drivers try to avoid smashes, while others aim to 'take out' their rivals by ramming them into the fence.

Chrysler Imperial 1964-66

Length: 6.2 metres

Width: 1.78 metres

Height: 1.4 metres

Weight: 2,050 kilograms

Chassis: Extra-strong truck-type chassis

Bodywork: Wrap-around 'O' single steel sheet

Engine: Up to 7.2 litres

Top speed: 200 km/h

The bodywork might get so bent in a crunch that it rubs or cuts the tyres. There's no time to lose – hit it with the sledgehammer!

Glossary

Acceleration

Picking up speed and going faster.

Christmas Tree

In motor sports such as dragster racing, a group of coloured lights that go on and off to count down to the start.

Disc brakes

Brakes that work by two pads, fixed to the vehicle, pressing on a ring-shaped disc that rotates with the roadwheel.

Forks

On a motorcycle, the two bars or rods on either side of the front wheel, which hold it steady for steering and suspension.

Four-wheel drive, 4WD

When the engine turns all four roadwheels rather than just the front two or rear two.

Gears

A system of toothed cogs or gear wheels which come together or mesh in different combinations, inside a gearbox, so a vehicle can go at different speeds for the same engine-turning speed.

Grand Prix

'Big Prize', one of the main events in sports like motor racing, especially Formula One (F1).

Navigator

In rally driving, the man or woman who sits next to the driver and reads out directions to them.

Pits

In motor racing, the garages and workshop areas where the cars are prepared for the race, and refuelled and repaired during the racing.

Rally

In motor sports, when many people with the same kinds of vehicles gather to form a parade or have races, especially along ordinary roads and cross country.

Stock car

A make and model of car that is mass produced for ordinary motoring, and which can be modified within certain rules for racing.

Supercharger

An add-on engine part that uses some form of air pump or fan compressor, driven directly by the engine, to force more air into the cylinders for extra power. Also called a 'blower'.

Suspension

The springs, pistons, levers and other parts that soak up bumps and hollows in the ground, so the people in a vehicle have a smooth ride.

Turbocharged

An engine with an add-on engine part that uses exhaust gases to spin a fan-like turbine, which drives a compressor to force more air into the cylinders for extra power.

Wheelbase

The distance between the axles of a vehicle, from the centre of the front wheel to the centre of the rear wheel.

Wheelie

When a vehicle rears up and its front wheel or wheels rise into the air, keeping the rear ones on the ground.

Find out more

Websites

http://www.formula1.com
All about Formula One (F1) racing, its history, the drivers, cars and teams.

http://www.ducksters.com/sports/nascar.php
Learn about NASCAR drivers, cars, tracks and what the technical words mean.

http://www.motorsport.com/photos
A huge collection of photos of almost all motor sports, from F1 to Champ Cars, rallying, motorcycles and everything else.

http://www.karting.co.uk
The website of UK Karting, the official British go-karting organisation.

http://www.santapod.co.uk/k_spot_difference.php
Part of the Kids Game Zone on the website of Santa Pod Raceway, the home of European dragster racing.

Books

This Is My Racing Car (Mega Machine Drivers), Chris Oxlade, Franklin Watts, 2006

Motorbikes (On The Go), David and Penny Glover, Wayland, 2007

Race Cars (Designed for Success), Ian Graham, Heinemann, 2008

Racing Cars (Motormania), Penny Worms, Franklin Watts, 2010

Racing Cars (Now That's Fast), Kate Riggs, Franklin Watts, 2011

Note to parents and teachers:
Every effort has been made by the Publishers to ensure that the websites in this book are suitable for children, that they are of the highest educational value, and that they contain no inappropriate or offensive material. However, because of the nature of the Internet, it is impossible to guarantee that the contents of these sites will not be altered. We strongly advise that Internet access is supervised by a responsible adult.

Index